Paella
like a Local

G.P. MANSO

Copyright © 2023 G.P. Manso

All rights reserved.

DEDICATION

This book is dedicated to all of my dear friends who taught me the secrets of making a perfect paella, just like a local. Your passion for this traditional Spanish dish and your generosity in sharing your knowledge have made this book possible.

I also want to express my gratitude to my beloved country for its rich and diverse culinary heritage. Spain is a land of healthy and flavorful food, and I feel blessed to have grown up surrounded by such deliciousness.

Last but not least, I dedicate this book to my mother, who instilled in me a love for cooking and a respect for the art of preparing food. Her guidance and encouragement have been invaluable, and I will always be grateful for her unwavering support.

Thank you all for being a part of this journey, and I hope this book will help you make your own unforgettable paella memories.

CONTENTS

	Acknowledgments	i
1	Introduction: The History of Paella and its Importance in Spanish Cuisine	2
2	The Essentials: Understanding the Ingredients and Equipment Needed for Paella	4
3	Choosing the Right Rice: Types of Rice Used in Paella and How to Cook Them	8
4	The Base: Making the Perfect Sofrito for Paella	12
5	The Broth: Preparing a Flavorful Fish or Meat Broth for Paella	15
6	The Proteins: Adding Seafood, Chicken, and/or Rabbit to Your Paella	19
7	The Vegetables: Incorporating Seasonal Vegetables into Your Paella	21
8	Cooking Techniques: How to Cook Paella Perfectly Over an Open Flame	24
9	Serving and Presentation: Tips for Serving and Plating Your Paella	27
10	Beyond the Traditional: Variations on Paella and Modern Interpretations of the Classic Dish.	30

ACKNOWLEDGMENTS

First of all, I want to express my gratitude to my Spanish friends from my hometown, whose love and support have inspired me to write this book. Thank you for always encouraging me to share my passion for cooking with the world.

I also want to thank my friends from La Coruña, where I have spent countless hours cooking and enjoying paella together. Your enthusiasm for this dish and your invaluable feedback have helped me refine my recipes and techniques.

To my friends from Palencia, thank you for introducing me to the diverse culinary traditions of your region and for teaching me so much about the importance of using fresh, local ingredients.

Finally, I want to acknowledge the many talented chefs and home cooks who have shared their knowledge and expertise with me over the years, as well as the rich culinary heritage of Spain, which continues to inspire me every day.

¡Muchas gracias a todos!

1 INTRODUCTION: THE HISTORY OF PAELLA AND ITS IMPORTANCE IN SPANISH CUISINE

Certainly, here's an example of an introduction chapter for your book:

Introduction: The History of Paella and its Importance in Spanish Cuisine

Paella is perhaps one of the most famous dishes in Spanish cuisine, and for good reason. This beloved rice dish, originating from the Valencian region of Spain, is a delicious and satisfying meal that has captured the hearts and stomachs of people all over the world.

While the exact origin of paella is somewhat unclear, most historians agree that it originated in the mid-19th century in the region surrounding the Albufera lagoon near the city of Valencia. The dish was traditionally made by farm laborers and peasants, who would cook it over an open flame using ingredients that were readily available to them.

In its original form, paella was made with rice, saffron, and whatever meats and vegetables were on hand, such as rabbit, chicken, and snails. Over time, as the dish gained popularity and spread throughout Spain, it evolved to include a wider variety of ingredients, including seafood, chorizo, and beans.

Today, there are countless variations of paella, each with its own unique combination of ingredients and flavors. Some of the most popular variations include paella Valenciana, paella de mariscos (seafood paella), and paella mixta (mixed paella).

BOOK TITLE

Paella is not just a delicious dish; it is also an important part of Spanish culture and identity. In fact, it is considered by many to be the national dish of Spain. Paella is often served at special occasions and family gatherings, and is a staple of Spanish restaurant menus.

In this book, I will guide you through the process of making authentic Spanish paella, step by step. We'll explore the essential ingredients, techniques, and equipment needed to create a perfect paella every time. Whether you are a seasoned cook or a beginner, I hope that this book will inspire you to try your hand at this classic Spanish dish and experience the joy and satisfaction of creating a meal that is both delicious and culturally rich.

Paella's origin story is deeply intertwined with the agricultural history of the Valencia region. The fertile lands around the Albufera lagoon, located on the east coast of Spain, were home to a diverse range of crops and livestock. As a result, the farmers and laborers who worked the land had access to a wide range of fresh and flavorful ingredients.

One popular theory about the origin of paella is that it was created as a one-pot meal that could be easily prepared by these farmers in the fields. They would cook rice over an open fire, adding whatever meats, vegetables, and spices they had on hand to create a filling and satisfying dish.

Another theory suggests that paella was originally created as a dish for Spanish royalty. According to this theory, a local chef created a rice dish with a wide range of ingredients to impress King Alfonso XIII, who was visiting Valencia in the early 20th century. The dish was so well-received that it quickly became a popular choice among the aristocracy and eventually spread to the wider population.

Regardless of its exact origins, paella has become an important part of Spanish culture and cuisine. In fact, it is often said that you can't truly understand Spanish food without experiencing paella.

Paella has also had a significant impact on Spanish cuisine around the world. Spanish restaurants in other countries often feature paella on their menus, and many chefs have developed their own unique takes on the dish.

Overall, paella is an iconic dish that represents the rich history and culture of Spain. By learning how to make authentic Spanish paella, you can experience the flavors and traditions of this vibrant country right in your own kitchen.

Paella is not only a delicious dish, but it is also a symbol of Spanish identity and culture. The dish has become an integral part of Spanish national cuisine, and its popularity has spread beyond Spain's borders to become a beloved international dish.

Paella's popularity can be attributed to its unique flavor profile and versatility. The dish is made with a wide range of ingredients, from seafood to chicken to rabbit, and each variation has its own unique taste. Paella is also a visually stunning dish, with a variety of colorful ingredients that come together to create a beautiful presentation.

In Spain, paella is often served during festivals and special occasions. It is a dish that brings people together and symbolizes community and celebration. In addition to its cultural significance, paella is also an important part of Spain's culinary history. The dish has been passed down from generation to generation, with each family adding their own unique spin to the recipe.

While there are many variations of paella, there are some key ingredients and techniques that are essential to making an authentic Spanish paella. Saffron, for example, is a key spice that gives paella its distinctive yellow color and flavor. Other essential ingredients include short-grain rice, olive oil, and a variety of fresh vegetables and meats.

In this book, we will explore the history of paella and its cultural significance in Spain. We will also delve into the essential ingredients and techniques needed to make an authentic Spanish paella. By the end of this book, you will be able to make delicious paella that honors the rich culinary traditions of Spain.

2 THE ESSENTIALS: UNDERSTANDING THE INGREDIENTS AND EQUIPMENT NEEDED FOR PAELLA

Before we dive into the recipe and cooking techniques for paella, it's important to understand the essential ingredients and equipment needed to make this iconic Spanish dish. In this chapter, we will cover everything from the type of rice to the type of pan needed to create an authentic paella.

Ingredients:

Rice: Short-grain rice is essential for making paella. Unlike long-grain rice, which tends to be fluffy and separate easily, short-grain rice absorbs more liquid and creates a creamy, slightly sticky texture that is ideal for paella. Look for "Bomba" or "Calasparra" rice, which are traditional rice varieties used in Spain.
Saffron: This spice is what gives paella its distinctive yellow color and flavor. It is expensive, but a little goes a long way. For best results, use high-quality saffron threads, which should be steeped in warm water or broth to release their flavor and color before being added to the paella.
Broth or Stock: A flavorful broth or stock is essential for cooking the rice and adding depth of flavor to the dish. Seafood broth or chicken broth are both great options, but vegetable broth can also be used for vegetarian paella.
Vegetables: A variety of fresh vegetables are often used in paella, including onions, garlic, tomatoes, bell peppers, and peas. Other vegetables like artichokes and asparagus can also be added depending on the recipe.
Meat or Seafood: Paella can be made with a variety of meats or seafood, including chicken, rabbit, chorizo, mussels, clams, shrimp, and squid. The type of protein used will depend on the recipe and personal preference.

Equipment:

Paella Pan: A traditional paella pan is a large, flat, shallow pan made of carbon steel with two handles. The size of the pan will depend on the number of servings you want to make, but a 16-inch pan is a good size for a family-style paella. The wide, shallow shape of the pan allows for even cooking and creates a crispy layer of rice at the bottom of the pan called the socarrat.
Burner or Stovetop: Paella is traditionally cooked over an open flame or wood fire, but a gas stovetop or outdoor propane burner can also be used. It's important to use a heat source that can distribute heat evenly and maintain a consistent temperature.
Utensils: A wooden spoon or spatula is essential for stirring and scooping the rice, while tongs are useful for arranging the meats and seafood on top of the rice.
By understanding the essential ingredients and equipment needed for paella, you can set yourself up for success when it comes to making this classic Spanish dish. In the next chapter, we will dive into the step-by-step process for making an authentic paella.

Rice is the star ingredient of paella, so it's important to use the right type of rice to achieve the perfect texture. Short-grain rice is essential for paella because it has a high starch content that allows it to absorb liquid and release its starches during cooking, resulting in a creamy and slightly sticky texture. Bomba and Calasparra rice are two of the most popular varieties of short-grain rice used in Spain for paella.

Saffron is a key ingredient in paella and gives the dish its distinctive yellow color and flavor. Saffron is one of the most expensive spices in the world, but a little goes a long way. To extract the maximum flavor and color from the saffron threads, steep them in warm water or broth for at least 15 minutes before adding them to the paella.

Broth or stock is an important ingredient in paella because it adds depth of flavor and helps to cook the rice evenly. Seafood broth or chicken broth are popular choices for paella, but you can also use vegetable broth for vegetarian versions.

In addition to the traditional vegetables used in paella, such as onions, garlic, tomatoes, and bell peppers, you can also add other vegetables depending on your preferences and the recipe. For example, artichokes, asparagus, and green beans are common additions to paella.

When it comes to meats and seafood, there are many options to choose from.

Chicken and rabbit are popular choices for meat-based paellas, while seafood lovers can add shrimp, mussels, clams, and squid to their paella.

Using a traditional paella pan is essential to achieving the perfect texture and flavor in paella. The wide, shallow shape of the pan allows for even cooking and creates a crispy layer of rice at the bottom of the pan called the socarrat. If you don't have a paella pan, you can use a large, shallow skillet instead, but the results may not be the same.

Cooking paella is a communal experience in Spain, with friends and family gathering around the paella pan to watch the dish come together. By understanding the essential ingredients and equipment needed for paella, you can create an authentic Spanish experience in your own kitchen.

When it comes to choosing the right pan for making paella, there are a few key factors to consider. The size of the pan should correspond to the number of servings you want to make, and it's important to choose a pan that can accommodate all of the ingredients without overcrowding. Traditional paella pans are made of carbon steel, which heats evenly and quickly, but you can also use a stainless steel or enamel-coated pan.

In addition to the paella pan, you'll need a few other pieces of equipment to make paella. A long-handled spoon or spatula is essential for stirring and arranging the ingredients in the pan, and a lid can help to trap steam and cook the rice evenly. A paella burner or outdoor grill can also be helpful for cooking paella, as the large size of the pan can be difficult to accommodate on a standard stovetop.

When it comes to preparing the ingredients for paella, there are a few techniques that can help to bring out the best flavors and textures. For example, you can toast the rice in the pan with a bit of olive oil before adding the broth, which helps to develop a nutty flavor and prevents the rice from becoming mushy. Similarly, searing the meats or seafood before adding them to the pan can help to create a crispy texture and enhance their natural flavors.

To get the most flavor from the ingredients in paella, it's important to add them to the pan in the right order. Typically, the aromatics like onions and garlic are sautéed first, followed by the vegetables and meats, and then the rice and broth. This allows each ingredient to release its flavors and cook to the right level of doneness.

Finally, it's important to let the paella rest for a few minutes after it's finished cooking, which allows the flavors to meld and the socarrat to develop. This crispy layer of rice at the bottom of the pan is highly prized in Spain and is often served as a special treat to the person who gets to scrape it up from the pan. By understanding the essentials of making paella, you can create a delicious and authentic Spanish dish that will delight your friends and family.

3 CHOOSING THE RIGHT RICE: TYPES OF RICE USED IN PAELLA AND HOW TO COOK THEM

Rice is the backbone of paella, and choosing the right type of rice is crucial to achieving the perfect texture and flavor. In this chapter, we'll explore the different types of rice used in paella and share tips for cooking them to perfection.

Types of Rice Used in Paella

There are several types of rice that can be used in paella, but the most popular varieties are Bomba and Calasparra. Both are short-grain rices that are grown in the Valencia region of Spain, where paella originated.

Bomba rice is the most highly prized variety for making paella, thanks to its ability to absorb liquid while maintaining its shape and texture. Bomba rice has a high starch content and a unique flavor profile that pairs well with the other ingredients in paella. However, it can be expensive and hard to find outside of Spain.

Calasparra rice is another popular variety for paella that's grown in the Murcia region of Spain. It has a similar texture and flavor profile to Bomba rice and is a good substitute if Bomba is not available.

Other short-grain rices, such as Arborio and Carnaroli, can also be used in paella, but they don't absorb liquid as well and can become mushy if overcooked.

How to Cook Rice for Paella

Cooking rice for paella requires a different technique than cooking rice for other dishes. The goal is to achieve a slightly al dente texture that's still creamy and slightly sticky. Here are the steps for cooking rice for paella:

Rinse the rice thoroughly in cold water to remove excess starch.

Bring the broth or stock to a simmer in a separate pot.

Add the saffron threads to the broth and let them steep for at least 15 minutes to infuse their flavor and color.

Heat a paella pan over medium-high heat and add a few tablespoons of olive oil.

Add the rice to the pan and toast it for a few minutes, stirring constantly, until it's coated in oil and starting to turn golden brown.

Add the aromatics, such as onions and garlic, to the pan and sauté them until they're softened and fragrant.

Add the vegetables, meats, or seafood to the pan and cook them until they're almost done.

Add the hot broth to the pan, making sure the rice is evenly distributed and the ingredients are arranged in an attractive pattern.

Bring the broth to a boil, then reduce the heat to low and let the rice cook, undisturbed, for about 20 minutes. Avoid stirring the rice during this time, as it can release too much starch and make the dish mushy.

After 20 minutes, check the rice for doneness. It should be tender but still slightly al dente.

If the rice is not fully cooked, add a bit more broth and continue cooking for a few more minutes.

Once the rice is done, remove the pan from the heat and cover it with a lid or a clean kitchen towel.

Let the paella rest for about 5 minutes to allow the flavors to meld and the socarrat to develop.

By choosing the right rice and following these cooking tips, you can create a delicious and authentic paella that will transport you to Spain with every bite.

To further explore the importance of choosing the right rice for paella, it's important to note that Bomba and Calasparra rices have unique properties that make them ideal for this dish.

Bomba rice, for example, has a very low glycemic index, which means that it releases its sugars slowly and steadily as it cooks. This results in a consistent, creamy texture that's perfect for paella. Additionally, Bomba rice has a higher absorption rate than other rices, allowing it to soak up the flavors of the broth and ingredients, without becoming too soft or mushy.

Calasparra rice, on the other hand, has a firmer texture than Bomba rice, which makes it ideal for dishes that require a longer cooking time. It's also known for its ability to maintain its shape and texture, even after absorbing large amounts of liquid, making it a great choice for seafood paellas.

When cooking rice for paella, it's important to remember that the rice will absorb the flavors of the broth and ingredients, so it's essential to use a good quality broth or stock. The saffron threads, which are steeped in the broth before cooking, are also a key ingredient in paella, as they add a distinctive flavor and aroma, as well as the traditional golden color of the dish.

The technique of toasting the rice before adding the broth is also important for achieving the perfect texture in paella. This step helps the rice absorb the broth more evenly and creates a slightly nutty flavor that's characteristic of the dish. It's also important to arrange the ingredients in an attractive pattern, as this not only adds to the visual appeal of the dish, but also helps to distribute the flavors more evenly throughout the rice.

Overall, choosing the right rice and following the proper technique for cooking it is essential for making an authentic and delicious paella. By understanding the unique properties of different rices and the importance of using quality ingredients, you can create a paella that's sure to impress your guests and transport them to the sunny shores of Spain.

When it comes to cooking rice for paella, there are a few key steps that should be followed to ensure that the rice cooks evenly and has the perfect texture.

First, it's important to measure the rice and water carefully, as this can make a big difference in the final outcome of the dish. A good rule of thumb is to use a ratio of two cups of water or broth for every cup of rice. However, this can vary depending on the type of rice being used and the altitude and humidity of the cooking environment, so it's important to adjust accordingly.

To prepare the rice, it's important to rinse it thoroughly in cold water to remove any excess starch or debris. Then, let the rice soak in the water for at least 30 minutes, which will help to evenly hydrate the grains and ensure that they cook properly.

When it comes time to cook the rice, it's important to use a large, shallow pan with a wide surface area, as this will allow the rice to cook evenly and absorb the flavors of the other ingredients. It's also important to use a high-quality pan that heats evenly and maintains a consistent temperature, as this will prevent the rice from burning or sticking to the bottom.

Once the rice is added to the pan, it's important to spread it out evenly and then let it toast for a few minutes before adding the broth. This will help to create a slightly crispy outer layer on the rice, which adds to the overall texture and flavor of the dish.

When adding the broth, it's important to do so gradually and evenly, stirring the rice constantly to ensure that it absorbs the liquid evenly. It's also important to use a flavorful broth or stock that complements the other ingredients in the dish, such as seafood, chicken, or vegetables.

Finally, once the rice is cooked, it's important to let it rest for a few minutes before serving. This will allow the flavors to meld together and ensure that the rice has the perfect texture and consistency.

By following these tips for choosing the right rice and cooking it properly, you can create a paella that's sure to impress your friends and family and transport them to the sunny shores of Spain.

4 THE BASE: MAKING THE PERFECT SOFRITO FOR PAELLA

The base of any good paella is the sofrito, a flavorful mixture of onions, garlic, and tomatoes that serves as the foundation for the dish. Making a good sofrito is key to creating a paella with depth and complexity of flavor.

To make a traditional sofrito for paella, start by finely chopping one onion, several cloves of garlic, and one or two tomatoes. Heat a generous amount of olive oil in a large, shallow pan and sauté the onions and garlic until they are translucent and fragrant.

Next, add the chopped tomatoes to the pan and continue to cook until they have broken down and released their juices. Season the sofrito with a pinch of salt and a few grinds of black pepper, and then let it cook for another few minutes until it has thickened and become slightly caramelized.

At this point, you can add other ingredients to the sofrito to customize it to your liking. For example, you might add red peppers, green beans, or artichokes to the mixture, depending on the type of paella you are making.

Once the sofrito is ready, spread it evenly over the bottom of the pan and begin layering in the other ingredients for your paella. The sofrito will serve as the base layer, providing a rich and flavorful foundation for the rice and other ingredients to absorb.

Overall, making a good sofrito is an essential step in creating a delicious and authentic paella. By taking the time to properly sauté the onions, garlic, and tomatoes, and adding other flavorful ingredients as desired, you can create a base layer that adds depth and complexity of flavor to your dish.

In addition to the traditional ingredients of onions, garlic, and tomatoes, there are many variations of sofrito that can be used in paella, depending on regional preferences and personal tastes. For example, some recipes call for adding red peppers or green beans to the sofrito, while others use artichokes or peas.

Regardless of the specific ingredients used, the key to making a good sofrito is to take the time to properly cook and caramelize the vegetables. This process helps to bring out their natural sweetness and enhances their flavor, which in turn adds depth and complexity to the dish.

To achieve the perfect sofrito for your paella, it's important to use high-quality ingredients and take your time with the cooking process. Use fresh, ripe tomatoes and onions, and don't be afraid to let them cook for a few extra minutes to ensure that they are fully caramelized.

It's also important to use a large, shallow pan with a wide surface area when making the sofrito, as this will help to distribute the heat evenly and prevent the vegetables from sticking to the bottom of the pan.

Finally, be sure to season the sofrito with salt and pepper to taste, and consider adding other herbs or spices such as paprika or saffron to enhance the flavor even further.

With a little practice and patience, you can master the art of making the perfect sofrito for your paella. By doing so, you'll be well on your way to creating a delicious and authentic Spanish dish that will transport your taste buds straight to the sun-drenched shores of Valencia.

One of the key benefits of making a good sofrito is that it allows you to build layers of flavor in your paella. By starting with a rich, flavorful base, you can then layer in other ingredients such as meat, seafood, and vegetables to create a dish that is both complex and satisfying.

Another important aspect of making a good sofrito is ensuring that it is the right consistency. The sofrito should be thick and spreadable, but not too dry or too wet. If it's too dry, you can add a little bit of water or broth to loosen it up. If it's too wet, you can let it cook for a few more minutes to allow some of the liquid to evaporate.

It's also worth noting that the quality of your ingredients will have a big impact on the final outcome of your sofrito. Use fresh, high-quality produce and spices, and opt for olive oil that has a rich, fruity flavor. These small details can make a big difference in the overall flavor of your paella.

Finally, don't be afraid to experiment with different variations of sofrito to find the one that suits your tastes best. You can try adding different herbs and spices, such as bay leaves, rosemary, or thyme, or swapping out the traditional tomato for roasted red pepper or other vegetables.

In summary, making a good sofrito is an essential step in creating an authentic and delicious paella. It allows you to build layers of flavor and adds depth and complexity to the dish. By taking your time with the cooking process, using high-quality ingredients, and experimenting with different variations, you can create a base layer that is truly unforgettable.

5 THE BROTH: PREPARING A FLAVORFUL FISH OR MEAT BROTH FOR PAELLA

A good paella depends on the quality of its broth. A rich, flavorful broth forms the foundation of a great paella, so it's important to give it the attention it deserves. In this chapter, we'll explore the key ingredients and techniques needed to create a delicious broth that will elevate your paella to the next level.

The first step in creating a great paella broth is choosing the right type of protein. Traditionally, paella is made with either fish or meat broth, depending on the type of paella being made. Seafood paellas typically use fish or seafood stock, while meat-based paellas use chicken, pork, or beef broth. Vegetarian paellas can also be made using vegetable broth or water, although these won't have the same depth of flavor as those made with animal-based broths.

Once you've chosen your protein, the next step is to start building the flavors of the broth. This typically involves simmering the protein with aromatics such as onions, garlic, and herbs, as well as other ingredients such as tomatoes, peppers, and saffron. The longer you simmer the broth, the more flavorful it will become, so be prepared to let it cook for several hours if possible.

It's important to keep the broth well-seasoned with salt and pepper throughout the cooking process. This will help to bring out the natural flavors of the ingredients and ensure that the broth has a rich, satisfying flavor.

Once the broth is finished, strain it through a fine-mesh sieve to remove any solids and ensure a smooth, velvety texture. The resulting broth should be rich and flavorful, with a deep color and a subtle complexity of flavors.

When it's time to add the broth to the paella, be sure to use it sparingly. You want to add just enough broth to cover the rice, without drowning it. Too much broth can result in a soupy, overcooked paella, while too little can result in a dry, undercooked dish.

In conclusion, creating a great paella broth is an essential step in making a delicious and authentic paella. By using high-quality ingredients, simmering the broth for a long time, and seasoning it well, you can create a rich, flavorful base that will elevate your paella to the next level. So don't skimp on the broth – take the time to create a truly memorable dish.

One important aspect of making a flavorful broth for paella is using high-quality ingredients. If you're using a fish or seafood broth, be sure to use fresh fish heads and bones, along with other seafood such as shrimp shells, to create a rich, full-bodied flavor. For a meat-based broth, use high-quality cuts of chicken, pork, or beef, along with bones and vegetables such as onions, carrots, and celery.

In addition to using the right ingredients, it's also important to simmer the broth for a long time to extract as much flavor as possible. This can take anywhere from one to several hours, depending on the type of broth and the desired level of flavor. As the broth simmers, it will reduce in volume and become more concentrated, which is what you want for a flavorful paella.

Another key ingredient in a paella broth is saffron, which adds a distinctive flavor and aroma to the dish. To get the most out of your saffron, be sure to toast it in a dry pan before adding it to the broth. This will release its natural oils and enhance its flavor.

When it comes time to add the broth to the paella, you'll want to do it gradually and in stages, allowing the rice to absorb the liquid before adding more. This will help to ensure that the rice cooks evenly and that the paella has a nice, even consistency. Be sure to stir the rice gently as you add the broth to prevent it from sticking to the bottom of the pan.

In summary, making a flavorful broth is essential to creating an authentic and delicious paella. By using high-quality ingredients, simmering the broth for a long time, and adding saffron and other seasonings, you can create a rich, full-bodied broth that will add depth and complexity to your paella. So take your time, be patient, and enjoy the process of creating a truly memorable dish.

In addition to the traditional fish or meat broths, there are also vegetarian options for making paella broth. For example, you can make a vegetable broth using a combination of onions, garlic, carrots, celery, and other vegetables such as mushrooms, tomatoes, and peppers. This can be a great option for those who don't eat meat or seafood, or who want to switch up the flavors of their paella.

Another important factor in making a good paella broth is the use of salt. Be sure to add salt gradually and taste as you go, as the amount of salt needed will depend on the type of broth and other seasonings you're using. You can also add other seasonings such as black pepper, paprika, or herbs such as thyme or bay leaves to enhance the flavor of the broth.

It's important to note that the broth should be hot when you add it to the paella, as this will help to prevent the rice from sticking to the pan and ensure even cooking. If you've made the broth in advance, be sure to reheat it before adding it to the paella.

Finally, it's important to use the right amount of broth for your paella. A good rule of thumb is to use about twice as much liquid as rice, but this can vary depending on the type of rice and the desired consistency of the paella. You can always add more broth as needed during the cooking process.

In summary, making a good paella broth is all about using high-quality ingredients, simmering the broth for a long time to extract as much flavor as possible, and adding seasonings such as saffron, salt, and herbs to enhance the flavor. By following these tips, you can create a flavorful and aromatic broth that will elevate your paella to the next level.

Another important aspect of making a flavorful paella broth is to use high-quality ingredients. If you're making a fish or seafood broth, for example, it's important to use fresh fish and seafood, as well as aromatics such as onions, garlic, and parsley, to create a rich and flavorful base. Similarly, if you're making a meat broth, it's important to use high-quality cuts of meat and bones, as well as aromatics such as onions, carrots, and celery, to create a flavorful and hearty base.

One key ingredient that is often used in paella broth is saffron. Saffron is a highly prized spice that is derived from the crocus flower, and it adds a distinctive flavor and bright yellow color to paella. To use saffron in your paella broth, you can soak the threads in a small amount of hot water for a few minutes to release the flavor and color, and then add the saffron and soaking liquid to the broth.

When making paella broth, it's important to simmer the broth slowly and gently, as this will help to extract as much flavor as possible from the ingredients. You can start by bringing the broth to a boil, and then reducing the heat to a gentle simmer and cooking for at least 30-45 minutes. If you're making a fish or seafood broth, it's important not to overcook the fish or seafood, as this can cause it to become tough and rubbery.

Finally, once the broth is ready, it's important to strain it to remove any solids and ensure a smooth texture. You can use a fine-mesh strainer or cheesecloth to achieve this. At this point, you can also adjust the seasoning and salt to taste.

In summary, making a flavorful and aromatic paella broth is an important step in creating an authentic and delicious paella. By using high-quality ingredients, adding seasonings such as saffron and salt, and simmering the broth slowly and gently, you can create a rich and flavorful base that will enhance the taste and texture of your paella.

6 THE PROTEINS: ADDING SEAFOOD, CHICKEN, AND/OR RABBIT TO YOUR PAELLA

The proteins used in paella can vary widely depending on the region and the cook's preferences, but some common options include seafood, chicken, and rabbit. Each protein has its own unique flavor and texture, and the choice of protein can greatly impact the final flavor of the dish.

Seafood is a popular choice for paella, especially in coastal regions of Spain. Common seafood options include shrimp, mussels, clams, and squid, among others. When adding seafood to your paella, it's important to use high-quality, fresh seafood and to cook it properly to avoid overcooking or undercooking. In general, seafood should be added to the paella towards the end of the cooking process, and it should only be cooked until it is just done, as overcooking can cause it to become tough and rubbery.

Chicken is another popular protein used in paella. It adds a hearty and satisfying flavor to the dish, and it pairs well with the other ingredients. When using chicken in paella, it's important to use bone-in, skin-on chicken thighs, as this will help to keep the meat moist and flavorful during cooking. You can also use chicken broth in your paella broth to enhance the chicken flavor.

Rabbit is a traditional protein used in some regions of Spain, and it adds a unique flavor and texture to paella. When using rabbit in paella, it's important to use high-quality, fresh rabbit meat, and to cook it slowly and gently to ensure that it is tender and flavorful.

In general, when adding proteins to your paella, it's important to cook them separately before adding them to the dish. This will help to ensure that each protein is cooked properly and retains its unique flavor and texture. You can also season each protein separately to enhance its flavor.

In summary, adding proteins to your paella is an important step in creating a flavorful and satisfying dish. Whether you choose seafood, chicken, rabbit, or a combination of these, it's important to use high-quality ingredients and to cook them properly to ensure that they are tender and flavorful. By carefully selecting and cooking your proteins, you can create a delicious and authentic paella that will impress your guests and transport them to the vibrant flavors of Spain.

7 THE VEGETABLES: INCORPORATING SEASONAL VEGETABLES INTO YOUR PAELLA

Incorporating vegetables into your paella can add both flavor and nutrition to the dish. While there are traditional vegetables used in paella, such as bell peppers and peas, you can also experiment with seasonal vegetables to add variety and depth of flavor.

When choosing vegetables for your paella, it's important to consider their texture and cooking time. Softer vegetables, like tomatoes or mushrooms, can be added earlier in the cooking process, while firmer vegetables, like carrots or artichokes, should be added later.

Some traditional vegetables used in paella include:

Red and green bell peppers: These provide a sweet, slightly smoky flavor and add a pop of color to the dish.
Onion and garlic: These aromatic vegetables provide a flavorful base for the sofrito.
Tomatoes: These add acidity and sweetness to the dish, and help to create a rich, flavorful sauce.
Peas: These add a sweet, fresh flavor and a burst of green color to the dish.
Other seasonal vegetables that can be incorporated into paella include:

Asparagus: These provide a tender, slightly sweet flavor and add a pop of green color to the dish.
Zucchini and squash: These add a slightly sweet, nutty flavor and a soft texture to the dish.
Artichokes: These provide a slightly bitter, earthy flavor and a tender texture.

Mushrooms: These provide an earthy, umami flavor and a meaty texture.
Green beans: These add a slightly sweet flavor and a firm texture to the dish. When adding vegetables to your paella, it's important to distribute them evenly throughout the pan to ensure that each serving has a variety of flavors and textures. By choosing and preparing a variety of seasonal vegetables, you can create a paella that is both delicious and nutritious.

To get the most out of your vegetables when making paella, it's important to prepare them properly. This can involve washing, trimming, peeling, and chopping them into the desired size and shape. For example, you may want to chop bell peppers into thin strips, dice onions and garlic, and slice zucchini and squash into thin rounds.

When adding vegetables to your paella, it's important to do so in the correct order. Softer vegetables, like onions and garlic, can be sautéed with the sofrito at the beginning of the cooking process. Firmer vegetables, like carrots and artichokes, should be added a few minutes later. Vegetables that cook quickly, like peas and green beans, can be added towards the end of the cooking process.

In addition to adding flavor and nutrition to your paella, vegetables can also help to balance out the richness of the proteins and rice. They can provide a fresh, light contrast to the heavier components of the dish.

When it comes to selecting which vegetables to add to your paella, you can either stick to traditional choices or experiment with seasonal varieties. For example, in the spring, you might incorporate fresh asparagus or snap peas, while in the fall, you might add hearty mushrooms or butternut squash.

Overall, adding a variety of vegetables to your paella can help to elevate the dish and create a well-balanced meal. By carefully selecting and preparing your vegetables, you can ensure that your paella is packed with flavor and nutrition.

When selecting vegetables for your paella, it's important to choose those that are in season and fresh. This not only ensures the best flavor and texture, but also supports local farmers and reduces your environmental impact.

Some of the most commonly used vegetables in paella include bell peppers, onions, garlic, tomatoes, artichokes, and green beans. However, you can also experiment with other vegetables based on your personal preferences and what's available to you.

To add extra flavor to your vegetables, you can also use spices and herbs. For example, saffron, paprika, and thyme are commonly used in paella recipes and can complement a variety of vegetables. You can also add a splash of white wine or lemon juice to brighten the flavors.

When it comes to cooking the vegetables, it's important to avoid overcooking them. This can result in mushy or soggy vegetables that don't add much flavor or texture to the dish. Instead, aim for vegetables that are still slightly crisp and retain their shape and color.

Overall, adding vegetables to your paella is a great way to increase the nutritional value and flavor of the dish. By selecting fresh, seasonal vegetables and cooking them properly, you can create a delicious and well-balanced meal that everyone will enjoy.

8 COOKING TECHNIQUES: HOW TO COOK PAELLA PERFECTLY OVER AN OPEN FLAME

Cooking paella over an open flame is a traditional and authentic way to prepare this dish. While it may seem intimidating, with the right techniques and tools, you can achieve a perfectly cooked and delicious paella.

Here are some tips for cooking paella over an open flame:

Choose the right pan: Paella is traditionally cooked in a wide, shallow pan with low sides, called a paellera. This allows the rice to cook evenly and absorb the broth and flavors.

Prepare your fire: You want to create a hot, even flame that will cook your paella evenly. Start with a bed of charcoal or wood and use a bellows or fan to create a strong, consistent flame.

Heat the pan: Place the pan on the fire and let it heat up for a few minutes. Add a splash of olive oil to coat the bottom of the pan and let it heat up for a minute or two.

Add your ingredients: Start by adding your sofrito and sautéing it until it's fragrant and slightly caramelized. Then add your rice and sauté for a few minutes until it's evenly coated in oil and slightly toasted.

Add your broth: Pour your broth into the pan and use a spoon to evenly distribute the rice. Add your proteins and vegetables in a circular pattern on top of the rice.

Cook evenly: Move the pan around on the fire every few minutes to ensure that it's cooking evenly. You can also use a metal spatula to gently lift and move the rice around to prevent sticking and encourage even cooking.

Create the socarrat: The socarrat is the crispy, caramelized layer of rice that forms on the bottom of the pan. To achieve this, increase the heat towards the end of the cooking process and let the rice cook undisturbed for a few minutes until the bottom layer turns golden brown.

Let it rest: Once your paella is fully cooked, remove it from the heat and let it rest for a few minutes. This allows the rice to absorb any remaining liquid and helps the flavors to meld together.

By following these techniques and taking the time to cook your paella over an open flame, you can create a dish that is not only delicious but also steeped in tradition and history.

Cooking paella over an open flame is a time-honored tradition in Spanish cuisine. It not only imparts a unique smoky flavor to the dish but also allows for the development of the socarrat, the crispy, caramelized layer of rice that forms on the bottom of the pan.

When cooking paella over an open flame, it's important to choose the right pan. A paellera is a wide, shallow pan with low sides that allows the rice to cook evenly and absorb the broth and flavors. Make sure the pan is sturdy and can withstand the heat of the fire.

In addition to the pan, it's essential to prepare your fire properly. You want to create a hot, even flame that will cook your paella evenly. Start with a bed of charcoal or wood, and use a bellows or fan to create a strong, consistent flame. It's important to keep the flame at a consistent temperature throughout the cooking process.

To cook paella over an open flame, you need to move the pan around on the fire every few minutes to ensure that it's cooking evenly. You can also use a metal spatula to gently lift and move the rice around to prevent sticking and encourage even cooking.

Creating the socarrat is a crucial part of cooking paella over an open flame. This is achieved by increasing the heat towards the end of the cooking process and letting the rice cook undisturbed for a few minutes until the bottom layer turns golden brown.

Finally, it's essential to let your paella rest for a few minutes once it's fully cooked. This allows the rice to absorb any remaining liquid and helps the flavors to meld together.

While cooking paella over an open flame can be intimidating, it's a rewarding experience that allows you to connect with tradition and create a delicious dish that's sure to impress.

When cooking paella over an open flame, it's important to take into account the weather and outdoor conditions. Windy weather can make it challenging to maintain a consistent flame and temperature, while rain can put out the fire altogether. To avoid these issues, consider setting up a sheltered cooking area or moving your cooking indoors.

Another important factor to consider when cooking paella over an open flame is the timing. You want to start cooking early enough so that you have plenty of time to let the paella cook slowly and develop the flavors, but not so early that your fire dies down before the paella is fully cooked.

In addition to the open flame, there are other cooking techniques you can use to cook paella, such as on a stovetop or in the oven. However, cooking over an open flame is considered the traditional and most authentic way of preparing paella in Spain.

It's worth noting that while paella is a delicious and beloved dish, it's not the only one that can be cooked over an open flame. Many other traditional Spanish dishes, such as fideuà and calçots, are also cooked this way and can be a fun way to explore other aspects of Spanish cuisine.

Overall, cooking paella over an open flame requires a bit of skill and patience, but the end result is well worth the effort. With the right equipment, technique, and ingredients, you can create a delicious and authentic paella that will impress your friends and family.

9 SERVING AND PRESENTATION: TIPS FOR SERVING AND PLATING YOUR PAELLA

After all the hard work that goes into making the perfect paella, it's important to ensure that it is served and presented properly. Here are some tips for serving and plating your paella:

Use the right utensils: Traditionally, paella is served using a large, flat wooden spoon called a paellera, which is used to scoop the rice and ingredients onto individual plates. If you don't have a paellera, you can use a large serving spoon or a spatula.

Serve hot: Paella should be served hot, straight from the pan. Make sure to time the cooking so that the paella is ready to serve as soon as your guests are seated.

Decorate with lemon wedges: Lemon wedges are a traditional accompaniment to paella, as the acidity of the lemon cuts through the richness of the dish. Place a few wedges on the edge of the paellera or on the serving plates.

Use a round platter: If you're serving your paella family-style, transfer the cooked paella to a round platter and place it in the center of the table. This allows your guests to help themselves and creates a beautiful presentation.

Add finishing touches: Before serving, add some final touches to your paella to make it even more visually appealing. You can sprinkle some fresh herbs over the top, arrange some cooked shrimp or mussels on the surface, or even use edible flowers for a touch of color.

Let it rest: After cooking, let the paella rest for a few minutes before serving. This allows the flavors to meld and the rice to set, ensuring that each bite is packed with flavor.

Serve with a smile: Finally, don't forget to smile! Paella is a dish that is meant to be shared and enjoyed with loved ones, so relax and savor the moment.

By following these tips, you can ensure that your paella is not only delicious but also beautifully presented. Your guests will be impressed by both the taste and the visual appeal of your dish, making your paella dinner a memorable and enjoyable experience for all.

When it comes to serving and presenting your paella, it's important to remember that it's not just about the taste, but also the visual appeal. A well-presented paella can be a feast for the eyes, as well as the palate.

One important factor to consider is the size of your paellera. Make sure that it is large enough to hold all the ingredients without overcrowding, which can lead to uneven cooking and a less appetizing presentation. A 15- to 18-inch paellera is usually a good size for serving 4-6 people.

It's also important to use fresh, high-quality ingredients for your paella. This not only enhances the flavor but also adds to the overall presentation. Choose colorful vegetables and seafood that complement each other and make sure that they are cooked to perfection.

Another tip is to use a colorful garnish to add some visual interest to your paella. Sliced lemons, fresh herbs, and edible flowers are all great options for adding a pop of color to your dish. You can even use the same ingredients you used in your paella as a garnish, such as arranging cooked shrimp or mussels on the surface.

Finally, don't forget to consider the setting in which you'll be serving your paella. A well-decorated table and some ambient lighting can go a long way in creating a warm and inviting atmosphere that will make your guests feel welcome and excited to try your paella.

By taking the time to carefully present and serve your paella, you'll not only impress your guests but also show them how much you care about their dining experience.

When it comes to serving your paella, it's important to remember that this dish is typically served family-style, with everyone gathering around the same pan to serve themselves. To make it easier for your guests to serve themselves, you may want to consider placing the paellera on a trivet or a wooden board, and provide serving utensils such as large spoons and forks.

In terms of plating, you can either serve the paella directly from the pan or transfer it to a large serving platter. If you choose to transfer it, make sure to do so carefully, using a large spatula or two to lift the paella out of the pan and onto the platter.

You can also add some final touches to your paella before serving, such as sprinkling it with freshly chopped herbs or drizzling it with a bit of olive oil. Another option is to serve your paella with a side of aioli or romesco sauce, which are both traditional Spanish accompaniments that add some extra flavor and richness to the dish.

When it comes to wine pairing, there are several options that work well with paella, depending on the type of proteins and vegetables you've used. For seafood paella, a crisp white wine such as Albariño or Verdejo can be a good choice, while a meat-based paella can pair well with a bold red like Tempranillo or Garnacha.

Overall, serving and presenting your paella is an opportunity to showcase not only your cooking skills but also your attention to detail and hospitality. With a few simple touches, you can elevate your paella from a delicious dish to a memorable dining experience.

10 BEYOND THE TRADITIONAL: VARIATIONS ON PAELLA AND MODERN INTERPRETATIONS OF THE CLASSIC DISH

Paella is a dish with a long and storied history, and while there is certainly something to be said for sticking to the traditional recipe and techniques, there are also plenty of opportunities to get creative and put your own spin on this classic dish. In this chapter, we'll explore some of the ways in which paella can be adapted and updated to suit different tastes and dietary preferences.

One way to mix things up with paella is to experiment with different types of proteins. While seafood, chicken, and rabbit are the most common choices, you could also try using pork, beef, or lamb. Alternatively, you could make a vegetarian or vegan paella using a combination of seasonal vegetables, beans, and grains.

Another way to change up the flavor profile of your paella is to play around with the spices and seasonings. While saffron is the most traditional seasoning, you could also try using smoked paprika, cumin, or chili powder to give your paella a different twist. You could also add in other flavorings such as lemon zest, garlic, or fresh herbs like thyme or rosemary.

In addition to these more subtle variations, there are also plenty of more radical departures from the traditional paella recipe. For example, you could make a seafood paella with squid ink, which gives the dish a striking black color and a slightly briny flavor. Or you could make a paella with noodles instead of rice, which is known as fideuà in Catalan cuisine.

Finally, there are plenty of modern interpretations of paella that take inspiration from other culinary traditions. For example, you could make a paella with Asian flavors by using coconut milk, lemongrass, and ginger. Or you could make a paella with Middle Eastern flavors by using spices like cumin and coriander, and adding in chickpeas and preserved lemon.

Ultimately, the possibilities for adapting and updating paella are endless, and there's no reason not to get creative and put your own spin on this classic dish. Whether you're sticking to tradition or venturing into new territory, the key is to keep the flavors bold and the technique precise, so that you can create a dish that is both delicious and memorable.

This chapter will explore the various ways in which paella has evolved over time and the different interpretations of the classic dish that have emerged. It will also highlight some of the key ingredients and techniques used in these modern variations.

One trend in recent years has been a move towards lighter, healthier versions of paella that feature more vegetables and lean proteins like chicken and seafood. These dishes often incorporate unique ingredients like quinoa or farro in place of traditional rice and may be seasoned with exotic spices like turmeric or saffron.

Another popular variation is the black paella, or arroz negro, which gets its distinctive color and flavor from squid ink. This dish is typically made with seafood, but may also feature chicken or other meats. Other regional variations include the arroz caldoso, which has a soup-like consistency, and the fideuà, which uses vermicelli noodles in place of rice.

In addition to exploring these variations, this chapter will also delve into some of the modern twists that chefs are putting on the traditional dish. For example, some restaurants are now serving mini paellas in individual portions, while others are experimenting with non-traditional ingredients like truffles or foie gras.

Finally, this chapter will address the importance of presentation and plating when it comes to paella. From the size and shape of the paella pan to the arrangement of ingredients, there are many elements that can impact the final look and taste of the dish. Tips for achieving the perfect presentation will be provided, along with suggestions for pairing paella with wine and other beverages.

This chapter will also discuss how paella has become a global phenomenon, with restaurants and home cooks around the world putting their own spin on the dish. From fusion paellas that combine traditional Spanish flavors with ingredients from other cuisines to vegetarian and vegan versions that cater to dietary restrictions, there are countless ways to enjoy this beloved dish.

Moreover, this chapter will highlight the role of paella in Spanish culture and society, particularly in the region of Valencia where it originated. Paella is often served at family gatherings, festivals, and other special occasions, and is considered a symbol of Spanish hospitality and warmth.

Overall, this chapter aims to showcase the versatility of paella and how it has evolved over time while remaining true to its roots. Whether you are a purist who prefers the classic dish or an adventurous cook looking to try new flavors and ingredients, there is a paella recipe out there for you. By understanding the variations and techniques discussed in this chapter, you will be able to create a paella that is both delicious and uniquely your own.

In addition to discussing variations on paella, this chapter will also cover modern interpretations of the classic dish. Chefs and home cooks have taken creative liberties with paella, experimenting with new ingredients, techniques, and presentation styles. Some have even deconstructed the dish, separating the rice from the proteins and vegetables and arranging them in visually stunning ways on the plate.

This chapter will showcase some of the most innovative and exciting interpretations of paella, highlighting the techniques and ingredients that set them apart from the traditional dish. For example, a seafood paella might be infused with Asian flavors by incorporating ginger, lemongrass, and soy sauce, while a meat-based paella could be given a smoky, barbecue-inspired twist by using smoked paprika, grilled chicken, and roasted bell peppers.

This chapter will also explore how the rise of social media has influenced the way paella is presented and enjoyed. Instagram-worthy paellas have become a trend, with chefs and home cooks alike striving to create beautiful and colorful dishes that are as visually appealing as they are delicious. This has led to the use of unconventional ingredients such as edible flowers, gold leaf, and even charcoal powder to add a unique touch to the dish.

Overall, this chapter aims to demonstrate how paella continues to evolve and inspire chefs and food lovers around the world. By staying true to its roots while embracing new techniques and ingredients, paella remains a beloved dish that will continue to captivate our taste buds for generations to come.

Another aspect to consider in this chapter is the regional variations of paella within Spain. Although Valencian paella is the most well-known and recognized version of the dish, other regions in Spain have their own unique takes on the classic recipe. For example, in Catalonia, paella is often made with seafood and served with aioli, while in Murcia, it may be made with snails and peppers.

This chapter could also explore how paella has influenced other cuisines around the world. In the United States, for example, jambalaya is a dish that draws heavily from the paella tradition, but incorporates ingredients and flavors unique to the Southern United States. Similarly, in the Philippines, the dish arroz valenciana is a popular interpretation of paella that features glutinous rice and is flavored with turmeric and annatto.

The chapter could also feature interviews with chefs who have put their own spin on paella, sharing their thought process and inspiration for creating their unique takes on the dish. This could include both professional chefs as well as home cooks who have developed their own recipes and techniques.

By including a diverse range of variations and interpretations, this chapter will showcase how paella has become a truly global dish, beloved for its versatility, flavor, and tradition.

ABOUT THE AUTHOR

G.P. Manso is a passionate food enthusiast and a native of Spain. Growing up in a family that cherishes good food, G.P. Manso developed an early love for cooking and a particular fondness for the iconic Spanish dish, paella.

With years of experience and a deep knowledge of Spanish cuisine, G.P. Manso has become an expert in the art of making authentic paella. Having honed their skills over countless family gatherings and community events, G.P. Manso has now decided to share their expertise with the world through their debut book, "The Real Spanish Paella: A Local's Guide."

In this book, G.P. Manso provides a comprehensive guide to making authentic paella, sharing their personal tips and tricks that have been passed down through generations of their family. With step-by-step instructions and mouth-watering photographs, readers will be inspired to recreate the flavors of Spain in their own kitchens.

Through this book, G.P. Manso hopes to not only share their love for paella but also to introduce readers to the rich culinary traditions of Spain.

Printed in Great Britain
by Amazon